D1715377

The complete step-by-step guide to a beautiful and inexpensive Hot Tub in just 3 weekends

BUILD YOUR OWN HOT TUB

Edward

by Ed Miller, and Steven Flamm

= 1936 -

TEN SPEED PRESS
Berkeley, California

For Debbie.
Without your love, patience and health
shakes, this book would never have
been written. Thanks.

Book and cover design by Fifth Street
Design Associates

Photographs by Edward Miller
Diagrams by Debra Flamm
The hot tub photographed and used as
a model in this book was built by
Steven Flamm.

Ten Speed Press
P.O. Box 7123
Berkeley, California 94707

Acknowledgements

We are extremely grateful to our
friends who allowed us to take their
pictures while they soaked in our hot
tub. Through them we hope to give you
some notion of the pleasures which
await you when you build your own
beautiful hot tub. And thanks to the
others who helped us in ways too
numerous to mention.

Lori Adams
Cathy Aroché
Dege Cole
Taffy Cole
Jim Dunlavey
Don Flamm
Lori Green
Jayr
Chrissy Karg
Joseph Lentini
Michael Logan
Rex Marchbanks
Donald Matter
Alice Miller
Charles Miller
Hugo Morro
Bill Murdock
Debbie Rhodes
Chuck Santacroce
Jennifer Shields

Permissions

We would like to thank Lea and
Febiger and the History Workshop for
their cordial letters of permission,
allowing us to quote from two very
interesting and informative books
published by them.

Dr. Richard Kovacs, A MANUAL OF
PHYSICAL THERAPY, Lea and Febiger,
600 Washington Square, Philadelphia,
Pa. 19106. (Fourth Edition), 1951.

Bob Gilding, THE JOURNEYMEN
COOPERS OF EAST LONDON.
Published by the History Workshop,
Ruskin College, Oxford, England, 1972.

A special note of thanks to Dr.
Magdalena Usatagui of Hoffman-
LaRoche for her patient and valuable
work on several scientific aspects of
the manuscript.

TABLE OF CONTENTS

Introduction

COOPERAGE

The piecework coopers at Shaw's spent most of their time on casks connected with the brewing industry, namely beer casks of various sizes, pins, firkins, kilderkins and barrels and occasionally, butts. The bulk of the beer casks were made from new timber, whereas the sugar casks, also made for the beer trade, were made from second-hand materials.

Revival of an Ancient Art

When you begin construction of your own hot tub you will be reviving an ancient trade, one associated with moleskin-aproned craftsworkers, sawdust floors, the dray-horse, staves and iron hoops. Some of the early tools used by American and English coopers to make tubs were the hatchet, chamfer knife, spokeshave, drawknife and froe. Your finished hot tub will be the kind of product a good cooper might have turned out a hundred years ago. As you hammer on the staves and hoop your own redwood, cedar or teak tub you will be reenacting all the routines once performed by the master coopers of early London and colonial America.

Pig Scalding Tubs

A century ago the cooper assembled casks for the wine and beer trades, pins and kilderkins to hold sugar and spice; he was responsible for making plant containers, furniture, brine tubs (the first refrigerators!) and pig scalding tubs.

The early cooper was a tradesperson who had to have a fine "feel" for wood. He had to be good at "getting his eye in," expert at assembling elements without blueprints and without using pre-fabricated materials. The cooper had to fit together wooden staves of many different kinds and sizes without using glue or nails. And he had to learn the secrets of the trade through a long term of apprenticeship.

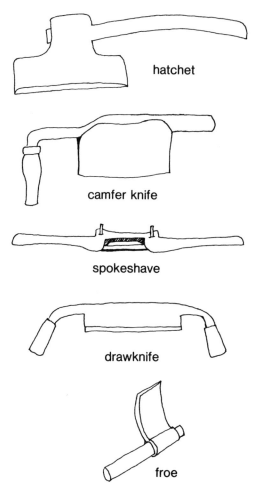

hatchet

camfer knife

spokeshave

drawknife

froe

Some tools used by early coopers.

Barrels of Rum

Interestingly, it was the rum trade which engaged the greatest number of early coopers. It is interesting to listen to the tongue-in-check description of one of these apprentices as he recollects some of the "dangers" associated with the cooper's trade.

There were other dangerous moments of course. They occurred when drawing rum samples with the vallinche or "waxer." The quickest method was to suck the rum up into the vallinche, hold it by placing one's finger over the end, and then by moving one's finger, to release it into the sample bottle. This method left the cooper gasping for breath if he went on sucking too long. Fortunately, however, others were generally around when sampling was in progress and a good slap on the back was always forthcoming when needed.

Incidentally, the term "waxer" for sampling the rum derives from the use of wax to make the staves slide on easily over the floor. A master cooper might begin his day by sniffing the air and, if he detected a trace of rum,

The cooper assembled leakproof wooden containers without using glue or nails.

might ask the apprentices what it was he smelled. "Wax sir!" was a common reply uttered innocently by the young apprentices.

Getting Your Eye In

The working methods of the early coopers were subtle and learned through experience. The techniques of cooperage were not contained in any single book but rather passed along from master to apprentice. An excellent piece of advice, as useful today as then, was for "getting your eye in."

Coopers do not depend on machinery, even though they use it. The main part of any cooper job is getting your eye in (coopering gives you a very good eye), setting your tools up, and finishing your truss [iron hoop].

The Cooper's Benchmark

The early American and British coopers were clearly workers with a strong sense of individualism. While the cooperage trade to some may have seemed artless and humdrum, those who diligently practiced it knew

differently. Every cooper was a skilled artisan who left his own personal mark on each vat or tub he built.

Coopering is still a highly individual operation. Each man has his own set of tools and has to keep them in condition. He works in his own individual berth. And the job when it is finished is his own. Every cooper has his own blockmark with which he stamps every cask he makes.

It was the combination of acquired technique, high sense of duty and personality which once elevated cooperage to the level of craft if not art.

The early cooper, his tools and equipment.

Chapter 1

HEALTH, GLAMOUR, PHYSIOLOGY AND THE HOT TUB

"Health, sex and glamour," were the words used in the *Los Angeles Times* recently to describe the hot tub experience. The author of the article pointed out that in the early seventies the hot tub was something known only to a happy few. Now, a decade later, more than 50,000 hot tubs are manufactured each year, assembly-line style, in cooperages around the United States. Moreover, a growth rate of more than 50 percent has been predicted for next year.

The Hot Tub Industry

Leaf through an issue of the *Wall Street Journal, Playboy* or *Penthouse* these days, and it is no accident to come across a full-page ad for the hot tub.

The hot tub industry is upon us. People like hot tubs and the entrepreneurs are bringing them to the masses. Buying a first-class ready-made hot tub today complete with redwood, hoops, seats, steps, heater, hydromassage jets, pump, filter, plumbing and so on can cost as much as a small economy car. The hot tub is no longer a bath in a bucket. According to *People* magazine, it's the place where deals are now being brought off. Business people no longer go to cocktail lounges to work out the terms of a contract; they soak with their competitor in their own customized redwood hot tubs where, according to *People,* they "melt hostilities into hollandaise."

The Drugless Tranquilizer

Those of us who are lucky enough to have their own hot tubs know that the hot tub is the closest thing to a fountain of youth to appear in recent times. The head of "Baths International" has called the hot tub a "drugless tranquilizer." Many doctors agree that the physiological and psychological advangates of hydrotherapy are real. What could be wrong with something which helps to relieve lower back pain, muscle soreness, many of the symptoms of arthritis, dermatitis, improves circulation, relaxes people and puts them in the mood for love all at the same time? Only the cost. That's why we wrote this book . . . to enable people to own their own hot tubs, to really help them to build one step-by-step for an affordable price.

Do It Yourself

Build Your Own Hot Tub is a practical do-it-yourself guide. If you want to see how much fun other people are having in their hot tubs there are a couple of good books available, *Hot Tubs,* by Leon Elder (Capra Press) and *Cannibal Soup* by Valerie and John Thompson (Chronicle Books). If you decide to get down to the serious business of building one of your own, from the foundation right up to the last hydro-massage jet, for a few hundred dollars—then this is the book for you. If you are still in doubt as to whether it can be done and whether you can do it, put your doubts aside. Instead of dreaming of buying one someday for thousands of dollars, build your own now!

With *Build Your Own Hot Tub* in front of you, you can easily build a wooden hot tub, the foundation slab, the total support system (pump, filter, heater, hydrojets, seats and steps)—the works—for about $500 (less, if you want to cut corners and build a smaller "soaking tub"). You can do the whole job in three weekends, by yourself or with the help of a friend. When finished you will have a hot tub as beautiful as you can find in any cooperage in the country. Furthermore, you will have made a solid contribution to your own health and happiness and to that of your family.

Hot tubbing for the health and enjoyment of your family and friends.

A Shirtsleeve Book

Build Your Own Hot Tub is a shirt-sleeve book which shows and tells you everything you need to know to build your own tub from the foundation up. We built our own hot tub, photographed *every step of the process,* and kept a minute record of everything we did in order to pass it on to you. We have eliminated what we felt to be unessential to the building process, concentrating only on what is important. *Build Your Own Hot Tub* can be used by the professional carpenter, plumber, or person skilled in using tools, but its fundamental purpose is to enable *anyone* to build a beautiful hot tub without having a specialized back-ground or practical experience in construction.

We suggest that beginners build the six-foot tub as shown. For someone skilled in the use of tools, however, our directions may be modified so that you may build a hot tub using different materials or by varying the size and the shape of the tub.

Savings

We have added, as an alternative to your using a gas-fired heater, a full chapter on solarizing your hot tub. Solar energy today is a totally viable alternative source of energy, hence a chapter on solar installation is important for many people. A solar heater may cost you more than a gas heater, but consider the payback time. Once the solar panels themselves have been paid for, the heat is *free!* Further-more, a number of state legislatures now offer an income tax incentive to people who opt to go solar. In California, for instance, homeowners who use solar panels to heat their hot tubs may qualify for a 55 percent tax break for using solar equipment.

Should you decide to utilize your hot tub for medical reasons, it is possible that with your doctor's prescription you may partially recover the cost of your hot tub through a health deduction on your income tax.

A word on geography: at present, there are more hot tubs out West than on the East coast. But you can build a hot tub wherever you live. The hot tub is *not* a fair weather friend. While certain modifications may have to be made to prevent the water in your tub from freezing in winter, your hot tub will function as well in Maine as in Mexico.

Physiology and the Hot Tub

There is a great amount of scientifically reliable information available in medical literature relating to the benefits of hot water and the whirlpool. The hot tub in many ways is a replica of the scientific apparatus used in the treatment of disease. The "model" hot tub we built and refer to in this book contains 800 gallons of water, is powered by twin hydrojets, and is capable of providing a temperature level in excess of 105 degrees Fahrenheit. Used prudently, and in conjunction with the advice of a physician, your hot tub can help to relieve the symptoms of a number of common ailments. Dr. Richard Kovacs, an eminent physician and an expert in the uses of hydrotherapy, summarizes the principles of whirlpool therapy in the following way:

The whirlpool bath is a most valuable treatment measure in a large number of traumatic and

Effects of Hot Water Hydromassage

Circulation	Local	General
Pulse rate	Unchanged	Increased
Blood pressure (arterial)	Unchanged	Increased
Blood pressure (venous)	Increased	Unchanged
Tissues		
Metabolism	Increased	Increased
Respiration		
Rate	Unchanged	Increased
Depth	Unchanged	Increased
Infections		
Local immunity	Increased	Increased

Adapted from: Kovacs, *Manual of Physical Therapy*, p. 28.

chronic inflammatory conditions. It is excellent for early treatment of stiffness, pain and sluggish skin circulation. *

Many people have discovered that the hot tub, like the therapeutic whirlpool bath, provides excellent and rewarding results. Proper use of the hot tub is excellent therapy for various forms of neuritis, joint stiffness and poor circulation. Hot water massage is often

*Richard Kovacs, M.D., A Manual of Physical Therapy. Lea and Febiger, Philadelphia, 1951.

used in modern clinics and hospitals to treat these problems.

Dr. Kovaks also discusses hydrotherapy in connection with the alleviation of pain:

> Local heating in mild dosage acts as a sedative on irritative conditions of sensory and motor nerves. This explains the relief given by thermal measures in many painful sensory conditions and in cramps and spasm.

The Vasodilator

The hot tub functions along the same lines as the medical hydrotherapy whirlpool. Your hot tub when heated to around 105 degrees Fahrenheit has a vasodilator effect on your body. Your capillaries, veins and arteries respond by widening in a natural effort to maintain normal body temperature. The effect is both pleasurable and healthful. Dr. Kovacs points out that there is "an increase of the rate of removal of local tissue products and in stimulation of the local resistive forces."

Circulation

When you step into your hot tub there occurs a distinct increase in circulation, metabolism and oxygen consumption, as well as a reduction of acidity in the urine and in the body's salt level.

All of these effects beneficial to your mind and body are carried out in the most pleasant way imaginable. That's hot tubbing!

Sex and the Hot Tub

Ernest Bruni who teaches Human Sexuality at the University of California at Los Angeles has said this of the hot tub:

> *When people get comfortable and relaxed nice things happen, maybe not necessarily erotic. The hot tub is an environment of pleasure.*

Alone and naked with your lover, experiencing the warm pulsations of the hydrojet stream, definitely creates a warm sensuous setting for expressing your deepest and most intimate feelings.

The Spiritual Community

By building your own hot tub you have opened a door to your health and happiness as well as that of your family. Your hot tub is in many ways like the hot water whirlpools used in medical facilities for orthopedic or osteopathic rehabilitation. However, hot tubs in and of themselves are finding increasing use by the spiritual community as well. The hot tub is sometimes used as a centerpiece for a number of methodologies involving re-birth, self-renewal and healing, or in conjunction with other kinds of therapy and forms of awakening.

The hot tub has received professional sanctions and is used by many retreats in the esoteric and spiritual communities as a means of promoting maximum relaxation; as an instrument to induce personal (or group) meditation; for creative healing; and, occasionally, for partial or even deprivational privacy. Testimony of users tends to confirm that the warm and supportive environment of the hot tub is a primal force in fostering loving relationships at many levels and can bring human beings into deeper, closer touch with themselves and with others.

For whatever reason you choose to build your own hot tub—as simple zone therapy by which to alleviate ailments such as insomnia, migraine, bodily pain or stress; or, positively, as an instrument for spiritual or natural communion; or simply for nothing more than to enjoy the mellow experience of soaking—the hot tub you build will give you and your friends a lifetime of satisfaction.

Chapter 2

THE SITE AND THE TOOLS

Selecting the Proper Site

If you are a homeowner, in all probability you will have little trouble finding a corner of your property where you can build and set up your own hot tub. The tub, base, steps and support skid will not take up any more room than a small patio or barbecue area in the yard—about 80 to 100 square feet. If you are a renter, you will have to discuss your plans for a hot tub with your landlord. You should convince the owner that the hot tub is an asset and in no way poses a threat to the property. This is how we approached our landlord. The promise of a little hot tubbing may also help to further your cause. If all else fails, and you simply cannot persuade him to take you on with your six-foot tub, you can always suggest building a "cuddle tub"—a diminutive 3 by 3-foot baby hot tub which would fit nicely into some inconspicuous corner. Incidentally, a hot tub may be placed indoors. Owners who live in cold climates have often opted to do just that. Hot tubs can be put in the darndest places. With a little ingenuity and daring, you will find just the right place for it.

Wherever you decide to put your hot tub, take a chair out to the proposed site and sit there for awhile to see how it feels. Look around you, think pleasantly of the days ahead and make certain that the site you have chosen is just right for *you*.

There are, however, a couple of limiting factors which you should observe when considering the site for your tub. Place the tub at least fifteen feet from your gas supply tank. If you are installing solar panels, the above rule naturally does not apply.

The supply skid containing the heater, pump, filter and chlorinator (optional) should not be right next to the tub for the simple reason that the pump makes a good bit of noise. Ten feet away will do.

The ground beneath the hot tub should be solid enough to support the full weight of the tub, water and occupants in wet and dry weather. For this reason we strongly urge you to build a concrete base to support the tub.

There should be no electrical apparatus nearby which could possibly come in contact with any part of the tub or surrounding area. The pump, if electrical, should have UL approval and should be placed far enough above the ground so as not to lie in water. A skid such as we suggest you construct should serve to avert any such eventuality.

In the Sun or In the Shade? A View from the Tub.

Location is of course a matter of personal preference. An open, sunny site is ideal for some, but not for others. If the view from your tub is spectacular, you should certainly take advantage of it. But it can mean a sunburn and being uncomfortably warm, too. There is also the matter of whether you intend to hot tub in the nude. Some hot tubbers do, some don't. But if you desire privacy, for

whatever reason, then you ought to consider some kind of enclosure . . . a surrounding arbor of evergreens, an attractive fence or simply situating the tub out of the line of your neighbors' view.

One of our hot tubbing friends put his tub high on a mountaintop; we placed ours in a corner up against a barn. In the morning hours we get the full light of day; in the afternoon we draw the shade. We feel we have the best of both worlds. If you are building your hot tub in a cold climate, and if you plan to use the tub during some of the cooler winter months, a good building site might be near a garage, against a shed, or close to the warm enclosure which houses the support equipment and most of the plumbing.

Integrate your tub with the environment. By incorporating the hot tub and equipment with your natural surroundings and beauty of your home, the woods, landscape and over-all setting, you will have significantly increased the value of your home.

Try to imagine yourself in your own hot tub. Have you chosen the right spot?

Surveying and Clearing the Site

Once you are quite sure where you want your hot tub to be, you are ready to survey, clear and level the site for building. For a six-foot tub, an area 8 by 8 feet will suffice. Prune overhanging branches with clippers, and with a rake clear away all underbrush and unwanted vegetation within the site area. Spade down a foot or two into the soil and remove any rocks or stones more than an inch or two in diameter. If you live in a cold climate, you know how frost can cause upheavals of the earth. The force of frost heaves can cause even the thickest concrete to break apart. Smooth out the area as completely as possible. The structural integrity of a good hot tub depends on its sitting level on a solid footing.

With a 24-inch carpenter's spirit level, check the plumb. A level has glass vials which show the vertical and horizontal trueness of a surface. When the bubble is exactly in the center of the vial, the surface is exactly horizontal or vertical, depending on the measurement taken.

Repeat each of the above steps to prepare a second area nearby for the support system. The support system requires an area roughly 5 by 5 feet in size.

In coopering the machine is subservient to the man rather than vice versa. Machines occupy a subordinate position. The cooper uses them to make his work easier, but they do not dictate to him what he does.

Tools for the Job: The Yellow Pages

With very few exceptions, most of the tools you will use to build your own hot tub are of the common household variety. It is more than likely that you already have a good number of them lying around the house. If, however, you do not have the necessary tools at your disposal, you can rent them. For about $50 you can rent every manual and power tool needed to lay the foundation, cooper the tub, make the seats and stairs and plumb the entire project from heater to hydrojets.

Get out your telephone book and look in the Yellow Pages under "Tools—Renting." In Santa Barbara where we live there are, for instance, no fewer than seven firms which appear under that heading. In a rural area you may find yourself somewhat handicapped, but within an hour's drive or so from home you will surely find a hardware or builder's supply store where you can rent all of the required tools.

Plan the tools you need for each weekend by making a list like the one on page 13 and rent all of the tools needed for a given phase of the job at one time. Start out early in the morning if you can and return the tools before closing time. Remember, you are charged by the day. If you return the tools late, you may be charged for an extra day's time. Take *Build Your Own Hot Tub* with you and show the sales clerk what you are doing. By looking at the photographs in the book, he will help you to obtain the exact tools you need for the job. Being unsure may cost you precious time driving back and forth to exchange tools.

Power Tools

While you could emulate the old time coopers and use hand tools for every phase of the job, four power tools will save you many precious hours and make the work a great deal easier and often more accurate.

The four power tools we recommend are: a 7-inch circular saw, a 10-inch table saw (the most expensive tool you might need, this saw rents for about $10 per day*), a portable electric drill and a sabre saw for cutting circles.

By planning your weekends method-ically you can do all the cutting of the redwood and all the dado work in one day and thereby keep the rental cost of the table and sabre saws to one day's rental.

Later, we will discuss certain procedures for using power tools in detail and, at the same time, discuss some cautionary measures to observe when using them. If you have reservations about using any power tool, we urge you to have someone who is skilled in using them help you get started.

*You will need it for only one or two days.

For the sake of convenience the building project has been divided into three stages corresponding to *three weekends*. A tool and material list precedes each stage along with an accompanying discussion on building that particular part of the hot tub system.

The three stages are (1) pouring the base (2) coopering the tub (including building the seats and steps) and (3) plumbing and heating the tub and support system. Other aspects of the project such as decking, solarizing, leaching and pH factors, are discussed individually at appropriate points in the book.

Chapter 3
The First Weekend

MASONRY

Tools Needed to Build the Foundation

☐ Pencil

☐ 12-foot tape measure

☐ Claw hammer

☐ Wheelbarrow or mixing trough

☐ Garden hoe

☐ Bubble level

☐ Trowel

☐ Shovel

☐ Carpenter's square

☐ 7-inch circular saw (or hand saw)

Building Materials Needed for the Foundation

Study the tool list and check off the tools you already have around the house. Plan to rent, purchase, or borrow the remaining ones. Then, repeat the same process with the materials list. Call or visit two or three lumber yards or hardware stores in an effort to obtain the lowest prices for these materials. Look around, talk to other builders, get in the car, explore. You will be amazed at what you can find for next to nothing. Be a scavenger! Remember that although you are going to build the best hot tub your money can buy, *you* are determined to build yours at the *lowest possible price.*

☐ Four 6-foot pieces of 2 by 4-inch "construction" grade lumber.

Since this wood is going to be used for the cement form only and later dismantled, just scrap lumber can be used.

☐ Two dozen 16 d. nails.

The "d." is a symbol for pennies. Nails are measured in the penny system. They were once measured in pounds. In rapid commerce, it became easier to say "pennies." A useful rule of thumb is to begin with a 2 d. nail—which equals one inch. Simply add ¼ inch for each additional penny. A three penny (3 d.) nail equals 1¼ inches, four penny (4 d.), 1½ inches, 6 d., 2 inches and so on.

☐ Three 90-pound sacks of cement.

☐ One yard of 50-50 mix (sand and rock mixture).

☐ Water (from a garden hose, for example).

☐ Twelve 8-inch anchor bolts (optional).

Constructing the Concrete Frame

Square off four six foot 2 by 4-inch Douglas fir boards. These will be used as a frame to contain the poured concrete. After the concrete has hardened the boards will be removed, so construction grade lumber is adequate for this phase of the job.

Trim two of these boards to 5 foot 6-inch lengths with the circular saw.

Since this is the first instance where you might be using power equipment, here are a few safety measures to bear in mind as you work:

Work slowly. Never attempt to force the saw. If you feel resistance, stop and withdraw the saw and find out what is causing the obstruction.

Wear tight fitting clothes while operating any power equipment. The tail of a shirt or sleeve flapping in the path of a power saw blade can be very dangerous.

Keep your fingers well behind and above the saw, always out of the way of the blade.

When you turn on the saw it should not yet be in contact with the work. Start the saw, *then* begin the cut.

Hold the work steady. Some carpenters who are experienced with power tools may not always elect to use clamps or a sawhorse to hold the wood being cut. However, those who are inexperienced are urged to do so.

After the boards have been squared off and cut, carry them to the site and place them loosely in a square. Push the ends together and nail them with duplex or 16-penny (16 d.) nails. Allow the nail heads to protrude slightly. Later, you will have an easier time removing them when the frame is dismantled.

Finally set the carpenter's level on top of the frame and check to see that the boards are level. If the frame is unlevel, pack some dirt under one end or remove some dirt depending on where the frame is off level. As an additional check, place the level across two corners of the frame and read the vial.

Cutting the boards with a circular saw.

Squaring the boards.

Putting the form together.

Nailing the form together.

The carpenter's level.

Checking the level.

Mixing the Cement

Bring the bags of cement and equipment as close to the building site as you can. Attempting to push a loaded wheelbarrow full of heavy wet cement across rough terrain is no fun. If you do not have a wheelbarrow, a practical mixing trough can easily be constructed by nailing a few 2 by 4's to a piece of 3/8-inch plywood.

The proper composition of cement is 1:3, that is, one part cement to three parts sand and rock mix (commonly called 50-50 mix). For every full shovel of cement thrown in the barrow or mixing trough, add three of the 50-50 mix.

With an ordinary garden hoe, blend the cement and 50-50 mix at one end of the wheelbarrow; at the other end, add some water. Gradually add water to the dry mixture until the consistency of the cement is just right. The cement is ready to pour when it is firm yet not watery. As you hoe through the cement, check to see that no part of the mix is dry before pouring.

Once you start mixing and pouring the cement, keep on going until the job is finished. The moment wet cement is exposed to the air, it starts to "set up" quickly, that is, the surface area of the wet cement gets crusty while the center remains wet. While there is no need to rush the job, just stick with it until all ten or twelve wheelbarrows have been emptied and spread around inside the frame.

Incidentally, try to pick a day which doesn't look too rainy. While a soft drizzle will not cause any damage to the fresh foundation, a heavy rain could cause problems.

It hurts to say so but we feel compelled to mention that you *could* cheat and have a cement truck simply deliver a yard of cement to the site and pour it into your frame in a few minutes. But doing it yourself is really easy, *much* cheaper, and the entire job can be accomplished in one afternoon.

As you empty each barrow of cement, push some of the mixture off into one corner of the form, and work additional pourings off into the adjacent corners. Stacking the wet cement in this way will delay the hardening process and give you the necessary time to mix and pour all of the cement yourself.

When a quarter of the cement has been poured into the form, use a section of 2 by 6 as a block to tamp down the cement, getting all the rock in the mixture well below the surface.

When the frame has been filled with cement use a 6-foot 4-inch length of scrap lumber to rod off the cement surface to eliminate excess cement and make the surface smooth. The task can be made a bit easier if you have a helper. Place the rod across two ends of the frame and, using a sawing motion, push the excess cement across the frame in front of the rod.

Mixing cement in the wheelbarrow.

Pouring the cement.

Spreading the cement inside the frame.

Tamping the cement.

Trowel Work

Use a cement trowel to make the surface of the foundation smooth. Using easy, semi-circular motions, tip the trowel slightly away from you as you work around the form. By holding the trowel too flat against the surface, the corners will dig into the soft cement and pit the surface, making it unlevel. Go over the entire surface once and allow it to set for about an hour. Repeat the above procedure once more, and again allow the cement to settle in the form for

Rodding off the cement.

The foundation, after troweling off.

Finished foundation, containing anchor bolts.

another hour or two. The cement will have begun to stiffen considerably by now. You can then return for the final troweling.

Anchor Bolts

Should you decide to sink anchor bolts into the foundation, this is the time to do it—before the cement hardens completely. Anchor bolts are L-shaped steel bolts which come in various lengths. They are threaded at one end. They are designed to be pushed into the wet cement and, when the cement has hardened, serve as "anchors" to which a deck or wooden platform of some kind can be attached with threaded nuts.

When the foundation feels thoroughly solid beneath your trowel and you note that the surface is smooth and free from foreign bodies, place a piece of cardboard on the drying cement to protect your level and check it once more.

In two or three days, the foundation will have completely hardened and at that time you can remove the framing boards. Pat yourself on the back. One third of the job is already finished!

Chapter 4
The Second Weekend

COOPERING THE TUB

Coopering was an important trade in the past. But little is known about it, and practically nothing about the working life of coopers.

Tools Needed to Build the Tub

- [ ] 7-inch circular saw
- [ ] 8- to 10-inch table saw
- [ ] Jig for cutting lumber (see page 23 for making a homemade cutting jig.)
- [ ] Portable electric hand drill and ³/₈-inch bit
- [ ] Sabre saw (for cutting out the floor)
- [ ] Surform plane or wood rasp
- [ ] Rubber mallet
- [ ] 1¹/₂-inch tape (such as electrical or duct tape)
- [ ] Crescent wrench
- [ ] Protractor (the inexpensive school variety)
- [ ] C-clamp
- [ ] Sawhorse (optional)
- [ ] ³/₄-inch dado set (optional—a router or chisel may be substituted.)

Building Materials Needed for the Tub

- [ ] 300 lineal feet of 2 by 6-inch clear vertical grain, kiln-dried, all-heart redwood, cedar, teak or other suitable kiln-dried wood for the tub, floor and seats.
- [ ] Four 18 to 20-foot ³/₈-inch to ¹/₂-inch diameter steel or wrought iron rods, threaded at both ends.
- [ ] Four steel or aluminum lugs. (See page 43 for making homemade lugs)
- [ ] Four 6-foot lengths of 4 by 4-inch "construction" grade redwood for the chine joists.
- [ ] 6 feet of ³/₈-inch doweling.
- [ ] 12 feet of 2 by 8-inch redwood for the steps.
- [ ] 24 feet of 2 by 4-inch "construction" grade pine for the support skid.

An industrial pallet can be obtained free of charge by scouting warehouses and factories. Machinery is shipped on such pallets and often discarded after loading.

Wood for the Tub

We are definitely friends of redwood when it comes to constructing the hot tub itself. There are, however, a number of other woods which may be used to make the tub, seats and steps (and cover). If you are not concerned about expense, you can use a number of exotic woods from which to make your tub, such as Philippine mahogany or Japanese teak. If, however, you are counting pennies, we suggest that you stick to redwood and other excellent woods in the lower price range. Just be sure that the wood you buy is either kiln-dried or has the necessary characteristic of swelling when coming into contact with water. Some of the woods which might make excellent hot tubs are: Douglas fir, Tennessee red cedar, Southern cypress, clear Louisiana red, Gulf cypress, several clear pines, juniper and even oak if it is properly milled. Redwood costs about a dollar a foot at this writing, and like most things in our society will almost certainly go up in price. But if you buy in large quantity instead of piece by piece (take a carpenter friend with you to the lumber yard; he can buy wood by the board foot for a much-reduced, wholesale price) and if you can buy the wood close to the sawmill, you can keep the rising prices well in bounds.

Grades of Wood

Redwood is classified and graded by using three criteria: clarity, appearance and freedom from knots. It comes in seven basic grades, ranging from the very best, —kiln-dried clear all-heart vertical grain—to the lowest grades where beauty and fine workmanship are not the prime requisites for the builder. The lowest grade is termed "merchantable." Incidentally, there is a considerable price difference from grade to grade. Buying the inferior grades can save you up to as much as half. A conscientious cooper, however, would choose only the top two or three grades of redwood from which to build

his or her hot tub. This would hold true too for any of the alternative woods mentioned above. The finished product will be far less likely to spring leaks, it will last a lifetime and it will make the best looking tub.

Swelling

Kiln-dried woods are strong, remarkably light and virtually free of moisture. This last factor is very important when it comes to building your hot tub. Kiln-dried redwood swells when it comes in contact with water. This swelling process constitutes an important stage in building the tub. Swelling of the wood causes the staves to eventually interlock to form perfectly tight joints and therefore eliminates the necessity of using glue or nails to hold the tub together. It is possible to use a hard wood, such as mahogany or maple, but far more care would have to be given to fitting the staves together than if you used a kiln-dried softwood such as redwood. As you will discover, the first time you fill up your tub there will be leaking, but very shortly after, the redwood staves will swell to fit, overcoming possible errors in workmanship.

There are ways of cutting costs on the wood without compromising on quality. You can kiln-dry any wood yourself. Simply store the wood flat in an attic or barn loft on pallets and allow it to dry out. This will take time of course. Another idea: buy your redwood as near as possible to the lumber mill—in the case of redwood, the Northwest; cypress, the South and so on. Another economy measure is to use a less than top grade wood (say, redwood containing a measure of sapwood), or even one which contains knots. In the latter case, make certain that the knots are away from the edges of the boards so as not to interfere with the butting together of the staves. For appearance sake, you can always sand the boards clean and put the knots on the inside of the tub so they are not visible.

Selecting the Lumber

When you get to the lumber yard, head right for the bins where the redwood is stored. In the storage part of the yard you will note that the wood is stacked upright in bins, usually in eight and sixteen-foot lengths. Kiln-dried redwood is remarkably easy to move around. It is comparable to aluminum among

Vertical grain redwood.

Sighting boards for straightness.

metals. Even a sixteen-foot board is relatively easy to handle for the average person.

Flop over each board while it is still inside the bin to get a rough idea of which pieces to cull from the lot. Put to one side pieces which show large knots, or knots which are too close to the edge of the boards. "Pin" knots—the tiny knots which appear on only one side of the board—are acceptable. A knot which appears on both sides of the board, however, should be rejected. Look for the grade marks "Certified Kiln-dried" stamped in

purple on the face edge or butt end of the boards.

Although the wood you will be buying is called "2 by 6" redwood, the actual ("dressed") stock measures 1½-inches by 5½-inches. This variation in size will soon become important when you decide on the size of your tub and how to put it together.

Another factor by which to judge the wood for your hot tub is "vertical grain"—the pattern of lines on the face of each plank which shows the annual growth rings of the tree. Wood

which has been cut tangent to the growth rings is rougher and flatter than cross-grained wood and will tend to have marbled appearance. Such marbled wood is somewhat less expensive than vertical grain, but satisfactory for your hot tub.

When you have selected your wood, remove the planks from the bin and lay them on the floor. Pick up one end of each board and examine it (by looking down the board) for signs of warping. Your eye will quickly tell you if there is any serious bowing of the wood.

Cutting the Wood

The 6-foot hot tub requires 45 4-foot 2 by 6-inch staves which will form the walls of the tub. You may use your circular saw to cut these boards to the proper length. However, to obtain an even truer cut, run each of the boards through the table saw jig. Use your carpenter's square to check the cut. Incidentally, it is a good idea to keep a constant check on each of your measurements whether you are coopering the tub, building the foundation, or plumbing and heating.

Making the Staves

You can, of course, build a hot tub just like ours, copying it to the very last detail. Or you can build one in your own style and use *Build Your Own Hot Tub* as a reference for one aspect or another of construction. There are certain basics which are, however, common to all hot tubs. For instance, the circular hot tub is, obviously, in the form of a circle, but the staves which form the circle (the circumference) are trapezoids. If you build the 6-footer (a tub 6 feet in diameter and 4 feet high), regardless of how you "design" *your* tub, you need a certain number of

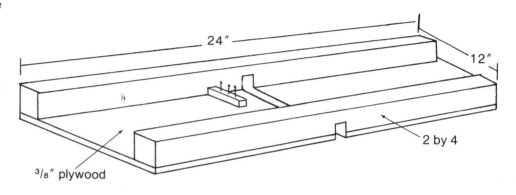

Plans for a cutting jig.

4-foot staves, you need to cut them correctly and you need to fit them together to form that circle.

First decide on the dimensions of your own hot tub. Consult the table on page 25 to find the number of staves you will need for the walls of your tub and then find the angle at which they must be cut so that they will fit together and form a sound watertight wall.

Angling the Staves

Each of the 45 staves (with the exception of the last) of the six-foot tub must be cut at an angle of 4 degrees 15 minutes (4¼ degrees). An efficient way to cut the angles is to set the saw at 4¼ degrees and run all 45 staves through the saw once, re-set the rip fence and then repeat the same procedure on the opposite sides.

Mark off the staves.

Run the boards through the jig.

Check the cut.

Setting the Saw

Table saws are equipped with an adjustable saw blade mechanism which tilts the blade through a 45 degree axis. The angle 4¼ degrees however, is too small to set accurately on the average saw. The way around this is to first set the saw somewhere between 4 and 5 degrees, make a practice cut, and then check the angle with an ordinary protractor. Continue to adjust the saw until you have arrived at the exact angle, then lock up the saw.

Incidentally, if the angle of the cut is greater than 4¼ degrees the diameter of your tub will be smaller than six feet; conversely, if it is less than 4¼ degrees the final tub will exceed six feet. Depending on the actual cutting

angle, you may end up adding or subtracting a stave or two when you finish. Later we will discuss cutting the last stave.

The next step is to cut the angles. When "ripping" (sawing in the direction of the grain) a piece of wood, it is important to hold the board firmly against the edge of the fence—the sliding metal guide on your table saw. To obtain a perfectly smooth cutting angle, keep one eye on the fence and the other on the blade while running the staves through the saw.

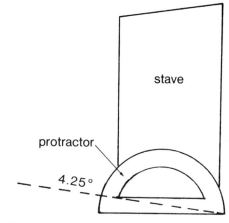

Use an ordinary school protractor to check the angles for every stave but the last.

Cutting Angles and Number of Staves for Building Various Sizes of Hot Tubs

Diameter of Tub	Cutting Angle	Number of Staves
3 feet	8° 30′	23
4	6° 30′	30
5	5° 18′	37
6	4° 15′	45
8	3° 6′	60

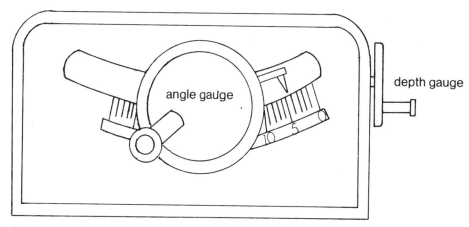

Table saw controls.

Ripping one side of the stave.

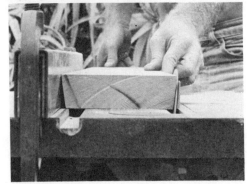
Ripping the opposite side of the stave.

The Dado

Grooves now need to be cut in the base of each stave. By means of these grooves, the staves can be attached to the floor of the tub, thus forming its sides or walls. The staves must be tailored to fit very snugly, so tightly in fact that it will require a sharp blow with a cooper's mallet to drive them over the floorboards, hence the need to cut these grooves or "dados" with great precision.

A ³/₄-inch dado set, although not a strict necessity, will definitely make the cutting procedure more accurate and speed it up.

Remove the circular saw blade from the table saw and replace it with the dado set. Adjust the depth gauge on the saw to ⁵/₈-inch and run the cutting jig through the dado as shown. This will create a ³/₄-inch slot in the base of the jig. Next, measure three inches from the right edge of the slot and draw a guide line on the jig with a pencil. Position a six-inch piece of ³/₄-inch plywood along this line and nail it in place, allowing the nails to protrude slightly. (You will have to reposition the plywood guide later.) Then, holding

Cut a ³/₄-inch groove in the cutting jig using the dado set. The dado set is a 3-blade saw designed to cut grooves or slots in wood.

each stave firmly against the wooden guide as shown, run all 45 staves through the jig.

Draw a second line ³/₄ of an inch to the right of the first guide line, reposition the wooden guide strip along the line and nail it in place. You are now ready for the second cutting. Repeat the same procedure as before and you will have created forty-five 1¹/₂-inch dados in the staves.

Use a wood rasp or file to clean the dados as shown. Be sure to store the staves indoors to prevent them from getting wet and prematurely swelling.

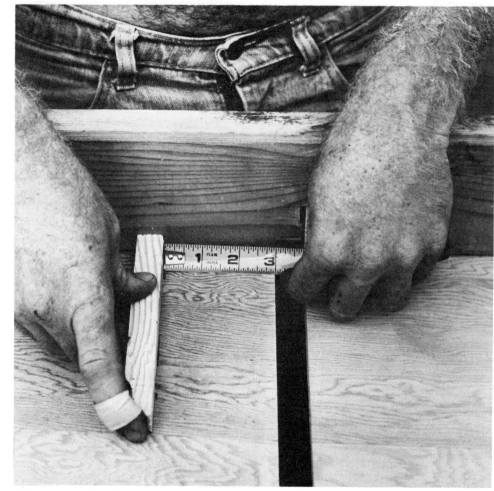

Setting up to cut the dado.

The first dado cut.

A half-finished stave.

Reposition the guide to make a 1¹/₂-inch dado cut.

The finished stave.

Filing the dado.

BUILDING THE FLOOR

. . . Having knocked his heads up, the cooper then marks the exact circumference of each end of the hogshead on to the heads by means of a large pair of compasses after which he walks to the nearest machine-driven band saw, switches it on and cuts round the compass mark . . .

Laying Out the Floor

If you look closely at the edges of the board you have carried home from the lumber yard you will see that the edges are slightly, nearly imperceptibly, rounded. This rounding took place when the wood was surfaced at the mill. To obtain thoroughly tight floor joints, it is advisable to run each of the fourteen floor boards (cut to 6-foot, 6-inch lengths) through the table saw one time to square up these round shoulders.

Ripping the floor boards.

Next, lay out the fourteen 2 by 6-inch boards on the ground as shown and mark the position for the dowels. With a pencil, indicate where the dowels should be placed. A suggestion is to place one in the center of each board and two at opposite ends of the boards three inches in from the ends.

An excellent tool for putting in dowels is a doweling jig. The job can be done by hand, using a manual drill; however, the jig will simplify and hasten the job. The doweling jig is equipped with an adjustable guide that permits you to align the cylinder over the exact center of each board. A clamp and depth gauge combine to hold the jig in place and to regulate the depth of the bore.

Marking the floor boards for dowels.

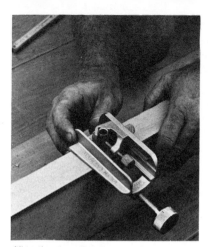

Align the doweling jig over the center of the board.

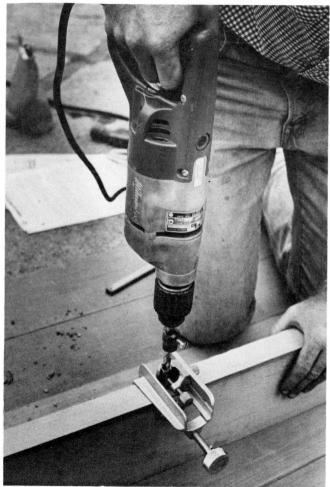

Drill the dowel hole.

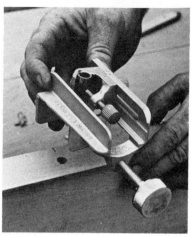

The finished hole.

Cutting the Circle

Drill a hole in one end of a three-foot piece of lath and insert a pencil in the hole. Drive a nail through the other end. You now have a homemade compass with which to inscribe a circle. Nail this compass at the center of the floor and swing the assembly around several times until the pencil line is well inscribed.

A quick and accurate way to cut out the floor is with the aid of a sabre saw. The sabre saw is designed for cutting circles and is easy to use. Simply remember not to twist the blade as you cut. The blade is slender and fragile and will easily snap if not held in a vertical position when being used.

Keep one hand inside the circle as shown and look slightly ahead and down on the guide line. Move the blade forward slowly and keep the saw just to the outside of the line. Most sabre saws have an adjustment which allows you to angle the blade slightly. By angling the blade just a trifle inward you can compensate for the slight outward movement of the sabre blade as you cut out the floor.

Insert ³/₈-inch dowel.

Pounding the floor boards together with a mallet.

Insert ³/₈ by 2-inch wooden dowels in the holes and tap them firmly in place with a hammer. No glue is needed.

An easy way to complete the joining of the floor is to place the floor planks on sawhorses and move along from board to board putting in the dowels and pushing the boards together as you go. Use a rubber mallet to hammer the planks together.

Inscribe a 6-foot circle on the floor with your homemade compass.

Nail a few lath strips to the smooth side of the floor to prevent the boards from shifting as you finish off the edges. They will also hold the assembly firmly together at the time when you have to move the floor into position on the chines and over the concrete base.

Use a surform, spokeshave or ordinary wood file to chamfer (bevel) the edges of the floor. Chamfering will enable the staves to slide on more easily when the time comes to assemble the sides and floor.

Cutting out the floor. Keep the saw just to the outside of the line.

Finishing the cut.

The finished tub floor.

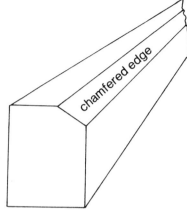

Chamfered edges.

Temporary lath strip to hold floor together while you work.

Completed lath stripping.

Chamfer the edges of the floor to make the staves fit on easily.

The Chines

The chine joists are literally the "backbone" of the hot tub. The entire weight of a six-foot tub, water and occupants is supported by these spines of wood.

The chines must be properly mounted to equalize the payload but also to permit proper circulation of air beneath the tub floor. Incidentally, it would be a serious mistake in our opinion to place the tub directly on the ground. The tub floor, if it is to last without rotting or leaking, should be well above the ground, free of water, mud, and vegetation. The chines afford precisely this separation between the tub floor and the concrete slab, provide a solid, dry foundation for the hot tub and insure the necessary circulation of air beneath the tub.

On the other hand, a small free-standing tub made of say, teak or 1 by 5-inch light cedar could be placed directly on the floor or on a wooden platform out of doors. Simply follow the directions for building a 3 by 3-foot tub. It may be plumbed the same as the larger tub if you wish or simply fill it through a hose connected to your

Space the chine joists 18 inches apart. Measure from the center of each joist.

bathroom fixtures.

Using 4 by 4-inch "construction" grade redwood, lay out the floor joists as shown. The four joists for a six-foot tub

should be placed eighteen inches apart. Measure from the center of one joist to the center of the next. Pencil a line on each side of the joists to mark their position on the floor. With pencil still in hand, mark the ends of the 4 by 4's where they are to be cut off. The chines should be cut off three inches from the ends of the floor. Use the power saw to cut them off. It will be necessary to turn the joists over and cut all the way through them.

Toenail the chines to the floorboards with 6 d. nails. Drive the nails in at a 45 degree angle. Drive them just far enough into the floorboards to secure the chines to the floor. Toenailing the chines in this way will prevent them from shifting position while the floor is lifted into position over the concrete base. Four to six nails in each chine should provide adequate support.

Turn the floor over leaving on the lath strips. Putting on the staves requires a good deal of pounding and the strips of lath will prevent the floorboards from shifting while this is being done.

Marking the angle of the chines.

Cutting the angle of the chines.

Toenailing the joists to the floor. (Nails can be removed later.)

The floor, complete and ready for staving, mounted on chine joists. This is a good time to drill the hole for the floor drain.

STAVING THE TUB

Attaching the Staves to the Floor

Once the floor is complete and positioned on the chines, it is time to put on the sides of the tub. Start at any point on the floor at the junction of two floorboards. Fit the slot of the first stave over the floor and pound it on as far as you can, first with the heel of your hand and then with a heavy rubber mallet.

Repeat this procedure with the second

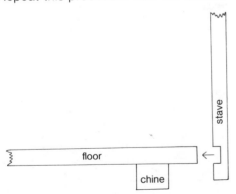

The relationship of floorboards, chines and staves.

Putting on the first stave.

The hot tub begins to take shape.

stave. Before you drive it on too far, however, strike the second stave on the edge several times, driving it snugly against the initial stave. Align each of the following staves in the same way as you work around the circumference of the floor.

Using electrical or duct tape, tape the staves together at the top as you move along. This will prevent the staves from sliding and shifting as you progress. In the next hour or so everything will start to come together and begin to look like a hot tub.

Taping the staves.

The tub near completion.

46 STAVING THE TUB

The last stave needs special treatment.

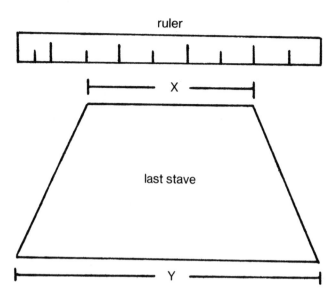

Taking measurements for the last stave.

You will discover that there is a gap into which the last stave will not fit. Because of a combination of factors—variations in cutting the wood, humidity, shrinkage, hammering on the staves, you will have to tailor the last stave to fit. Even though your mathematical calculations are unimpeachable, there is simply no practical way to avoid these limitations when coopering the walls of the tub.

To make the last stave, four measurements are necessary. Measure the opening of the final gap at the top and at the bottom. This will give you the width (w) your last stave must be. Then take an inside (x) and outside (y) measurement of this same gap to determine the final angle. Simply re-set the table saw and cut the last stave. It will fit perfectly.

HOOPING THE TUB

Hoops and Lugs

Four 19- to 20-foot $\frac{3}{8}$-inch flexible steel (or round, wrought iron) hoops threaded at both ends are required to encircle and support the staves. In addition, you will have to buy or make four lugs to join the hoops together. Should you encounter difficulty in finding a single hoop 20 feet in length, you could, of course, combine two shorter hoops and double the number of lugs.

A plan for making your own lugs is included on page 43. A simple square piece of aluminum and a bit for boring metal is all that is required.

Instead of the usual steel cables sold by cooperages or barrel makers for this purpose, you might try using thin aluminum bands—the kind used by some manufacturers to secure wooden crates that contain heavy machinery. Another alternative is to use $\frac{1}{2}$-inch to

Connecting the first hoop and lug.

$\frac{3}{8}$-inch flexible cables to hoop your tub—the kind, for instance, used by the telephone company to erect telephone poles. In any case, some method of strongly securing the staves is important because of the considerable water pressure against them. Water

pressure in your hot tub increases with depth. For example, although the pressure near the top of the six-foot tub is only 31 lbs per square foot, the water pressure at the bottom of the tub is 218 lbs per square foot, pressing equally in every direction on the side

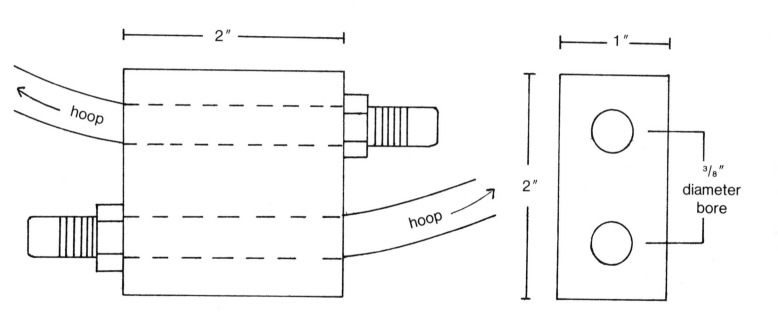

An easy-to-make aluminum lug to secure the tub hoops.

walls of the tub. Therefore, strong bracing near the base of the tub is critical. The arrangement of hoops suggested further on has been reliably worked out to assure optimum support for the entire tub.

Connect the first hoop and lug as shown, pass it over the top of the staves, and force it down to a point opposite the floor boards. (Find the center of the floor and use a ruler to mark the position of the floor on the outside of the tub.) Be certain that the hoop is parallel to the floor all the way around the tub. Next, tighten the nuts on the lug with a small crescent wrench. Tighten them just enough to keep the hoop from slipping. Over-tightening them too soon will make it difficult to balance the tension on all four hoops once they are in place.

Place the second hoop fourteen inches from the base of the tub. The third and fourth hoops should be placed respectively twenty-eight and forty-four inches above the base.

Placing the first hoop in parallel with the floor boards.

Hand-tighten the first hoop.

Use a tape measure to properly space the hoops.

Finishing

Finally, strip the duct tape away from the tops of the staves and, with a machine sander (we used a Rockwell belt sander) or piece of sandpaper wrapped around a wood block, finish off all the rough spots on the tub. Chamfer the ends of the staves. There will be a lot of climbing in and out and perching on the edge of the tub in the months ahead. It is, therefore, important to sand and round the ends of the staves with care.

Sanding the ends of the staves.

The finished tub.

BUILDING THE SEATS AND STEPS

The next step is to construct a pair of inside seats. It is now time to decide on a "blower," "hydro-massage jets" or both. The tub in *Build Your Own Hot Tub* is equipped with two powerful pulsating hydrojets which were installed in the side walls of the tub. You may elect instead to install a supercharger and blower. This apparatus consists of a plastic ring which lies coiled on the inside edge of the floor of the tub. Should you install a blower, it might be a good idea to construct latticed seats to permit the water from the ring to bubble upward *through* and around the seats. With hydrojets installed in the walls of the tub, simple solid wooden benches are all that are required.

Incidentally, there is no reason why both seats must be the same height. If you have small children in your family, place one of the seats nearer to the top of the tub and the other seat low enough to permit you to sit immersed to the chin in hot water.

Making the Seats

When you have made up your mind where you want to put the seats, place a six-foot piece of 2 by 8-inch redwood across one end of the tub. Mark off the ends with a pencil using the inside edge of the tub as a straightedge. Cut off the ends and you have the first seat. Repeat the same procedure once more to make the second seat.

From pieces of scrap lumber remaining after cutting out the seats, cut off four sections for the ledgers, each one an inch in width. These end pieces have already been cut at the proper angles and may therefore be used to support the seats. Using 1½-inch wood screws, attach the ledgers to the inside tub wall. With one-inch screws, fasten the benches to the ledgers. Use the tip of the drill bit to countersink the screws and some fine sand-paper wrapped around a block of wood to smooth off the seats.

Marking the seat to length and angle.

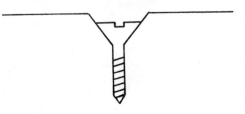

Countersink the screws for the seats.

Screw in the ledger for the tub seats.

The seats installed.

Wooden Steps

This is a job you may prefer to put off until a rainy day or until a weekday evening after the plumbing has been done. Building a set of steps is easy and can be accomplished in a couple of hours. Naturally, if you decide to sink your tub into a deck or in any way place it below the ground level, wooden steps will not be necessary.

Start with two six-foot pieces of 2 by 6-inch redwood to make the side rails of the steps. Lean one rail board against the tub and adjust it to a suitable angle. Place the carpenter's level against the board and, holding it parallel to the sides of the tub, check the vial to see that it is vertical. Using the edge of the level as a straightedge, draw a cutting line on the rail. Cut the board and use it as a pattern to make the second step rail.

Cut four 18-inch pieces of 2 by 6-inch redwood and square them off. Sandwich them evenly between the two side rails and mark their position with a pencil. Use the level to verify that they are parallel. Nail the steps to the rails with galvanized 8 d. nails.

Cut a curve with the sabre saw in the top step. This curve should coincide with the circumference of the tub and will allow the stair assembly to fit snugly against the side of the tub and it will also give it a customized appearance.

Making the side rail for the steps.

Nailing the steps together with 8 d. galvanized nails.

Completing the steps assembly.

Chapter 5
The Third Weekend

PLUMBING THE TUB

Tools for Plumbing and Heating

- [ ] Portable electric hand drill
- [ ] Hole saw—2⁵/₁₆-inch diameter
- [ ] Hand pipe cutter for copper pipe. (An ordinary hand saw can be used to cut PVC pipe.)
- [ ] Small hand-held propane torch
- [ ] Soldering paste
- [ ] Solder
- [ ] ¹/₂-inch teflon tape
- [ ] Screwdriver
- [ ] Emery cloth

Building Materials for Plumbing and Heating the Tub

- [ ] Heater (gas, solar, wood, other).
- [ ] ³/₄- to one-horsepower electrical water pump.
- [ ] Water filter.
- [ ] PVC or copper pipe (1 to 1³/₈-inches in diameter).

  Note: You may use all copper tubing to plumb your hot tub, all PVC (poly-vinyl-chloride) or a mixture of the two. We prefer PVC because of its characteristics (it is extraordinarily lightweight, heat-resistant, strong but can be cut with a hand saw and easily interconnected using only a liquid weld-on) and because of its relatively low cost. However, we decided to combine the two materials in our model hot tub to provide users of either material with information on how to use one or the other.

- [ ] 6-inch section of one-inch PVC.
- [ ] 1³/₈-inch rubber fuel line.

  The amount of PVC and rubber fuel line will depend on the distance between the tub and the support system.

- [ ] Hose bib.
- [ ] PVC elbows.
- [ ] PVC threaded ring adapter.
- [ ] PVC shut-off valve.
- [ ] ³/₄-inch galvanized pipe.
- [ ] 2⁵/₁₆-inch drain valve.
- [ ] 2⁵/₁₆-inch inlet valve.
- [ ] 2⁵/₁₆-inch suction outlet.
- [ ] One hydromassage unit and two jet valves.
- [ ] Eight auto radiator clamps.
- [ ] Soldering paste for copper welds.
- [ ] Liquid weld for PVC.

Installing the Drain

Start the plumbing system or loop by drilling a 2⁵/₁₆-inch port about six inches in from the edge of the tub. Although there are several tools with which the job might be done, a "hole saw" which will fit your electrical drill is ideal for this purpose.

The best time to do this is before the tub is connected in any way to the support skid and while you can still turn the tub on its side to be able to easily reach the bottom.

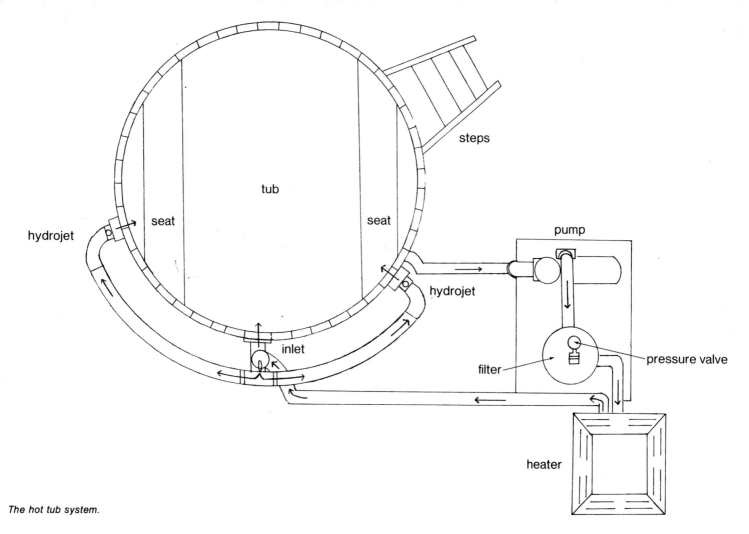

The hot tub system.

A word about using the hole saw: drill three-quarters the way through the tub floor, stop and drill through from the other side. Attempting to go all the way through the first time may cause the wood to splinter or the board to split. With the tub still on its side, install the drain. Wrap a layer of teflon around the threaded part of the drain; swab the threads with a liquid PVC weld and screw the valve into the nut through the hole in the tub floor. The "eyeball" of the drain should face inside the tub, and the nut should be on the outside of the floor. First, hand tighten the nut, then use a crescent wrench to tighten it more securely. Be careful not to over-tighten the nut and break the threads on the assembly. The combination of teflon and sealant will make the drain waterproof and when the sealant dries, will provide a permanent seal.

Fit a PVC elbow, a short straight piece of plastic pipe and a hose bib to the drain and you have completed the job.

Hose bib and floor drain assembly for draining the tub.

Wrap a layer of teflon tape around the drain valve.

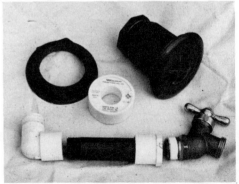

One kind of drain assembly for your hot tub.

The Support System

Return the tub to an upright position. Set the tub squarely on the foundation, checking its horizontal and vertical position with a level. You are ready to install the hot water inlet.

The Hot Water Inlet Port

Repeat the procedure for installing the drain when drilling the hot water inlet port. This port should be placed 26 to 30 inches above the floor and on the side nearest the heater.

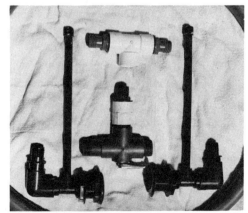

The hydrojet assembly.

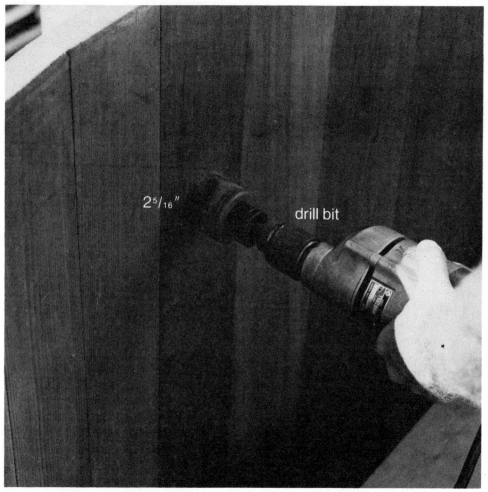

$2\frac{5}{16}''$ drill bit

Drilling one of the 5 ports (drain, inlet and outlet, 2 hydrojet ports) of the hot tub.

104986088

The Suction Drain Port

A third hole the same size as the others should be drilled six to eight inches above the floor on the side nearest the pump to house the suction drain assembly.

The Hydrojet Ports

After you decide where you want to put the two hydrojets, drill two additional holes 2⁵/₁₆ inches in diameter. In our tub we centered one jet eight inches above one seat and the second, twelve inches above the other. The hydrojet assembly consists of (1) two massage jets and their vertical air intake pipes, (2) an inlet control connected to the heater line used for filling and heating the tub and (3) a manifold unit which shunts the water entering the inlet to both hydro-massage jets. The shunt is activated by turning a brass gate control on top of the manifold unit.

The Heater

There are many ways by which you can heat your hot tub. Two of the more efficient and least costly methods are by means of a gas heater or by the more modern method of solar energy.

One friend of ours heated his hot tub in a rather innovative way. He dismantled the hood of an old 1941 four-door Packard, filled it with water, coiled up fifty feet of narrow copper tubing inside the hood, put the whole thing up on cement blocks and heated it by wood. Using a tiny water pump he circulated the hot water through his hot tub. It worked pretty well, too! This is just to point out that there are many ingenious ways by which you could heat your tub once you start thinking about it.

We decided on a more conventional source of energy—a gas heater—for three reasons. First, we were looking for a heater which was capable of heating up the tub *quickly*. Secondly, we wanted to *outlay the least capital possible* and thirdly, we wanted a *low-cost energy* source once the initial investment had been made.

We bought a used pool heater from a swimming pool contractor for $40. At that price we gave up our previous thoughts of going solar—which is a way of getting *free heat*. After buying two solar panels (an investment of approximately $300), there is no further cost for energy. It is a perfectly viable alternative to using any of the conventional fossil fuel machines. For that reason we decided to add a chapter to show you how to fit your hot tub system with solar collectors.

We suggest that you shop around as we did for a gas heater in the event that you do not decide to "go solar." It is incredible the number of used heaters of this kind which are floating around plumbing shops and rusting away in junkyards. The one we purchased for $40 worked fine except for a cracked firewall—the asbestos wall located in the combustion chamber of the heater. Once that was replaced, the heater ran perfectly. Now that our heater is hooked up and running we are more than ever convinced that a swimming pool heater (designed to heat large quantities of water) is ideal for the job of heating a hot tub containing only 800 gallons of water. Ordinarily, this kind of heater would take a day or so to heat a swimming pool, but in *less than a half hour* it can heat your hot tub to 105 degrees Fahrenheit! Many of the other alternatives for heating your tub pale by comparison with that kind of efficiency.

Formula for Heat

Heat is measured in BTU's—British Thermal Units. One BTU represents the amount of heat required to raise one pound of water one degree Fahrenheit. The six-foot hot tub, when filled, contains 800 gallons of water. A gallon of water weighs slightly more than eight pounds. Your heater is therefore required to heat a total of 6400 pounds of water.

During the warmer months, water which is just sitting in your tub may measure between 75 and 85 degrees F. The goal is to heat these 6400 pounds 20 degrees. This 20 degree difference in temperature (called delta t, Δt, by engineers) is the difference between the ambient (outdoor) temperature of 85 degrees and the desired temperature of 105 degrees. To determine the capacity of the heater needed to accomplish this job, the heating need must be expressed in BTU's. Multiply the 6400 pounds of water in the tub by the delta t (the above result is 128,000 BTU's in this example) and that is the number of BTU's your heater must be able to generate in a given time period. Look at the Table on page 58 and you will be able to "engineer" your own heating system depending on where you live.

In addition to the capacity of your heater, it should have a sound recovery rate—that is, be able to adequately compensate for various types of heat loss while the hot tub is in use.

Heat Loss

A hot tub loses heat in several ways—by heat lost to the outside air (about 5 degrees per hour under normal conditions), by absorption of heat by the occupants of the tub (another 5 degrees per hour) and finally by heat dissipated through the hydrojets (5 to 7 degrees per hour). A thermostat on your heater will allow it to "recover" this heat drain while you soak comfortably in the tub. It will consequently maintain a constant tub temperature.

Cost

The cost of fuel to heat your hot tub by gas is small. For example, if you use the heater a half-hour per day (average use), it will cost about fifty cents a day. Electric heaters are initially less expensive to buy but quite expensive to operate. Also a 12 KW (Kilowatt) electric heater requires a main power source of 60 amps. Most home power systems are only 15 amps in capacity and require considerable beefing-up electrically in order to generate sufficient and safe power. Unless you are versatile enough to change over your house current yourself, an electrical contractor might charge as much as a few hundred dollars to do the job.

Summer Conditions

Raising the water in the hot tub from 85° F. to 105° F.
Heat required: 128,000 BTU

Type of Heater	Time Required to 105° F.
60,000 BTU/hr	2 hours
120,000 BTU/hr	1 hour
180,000 BTU/hr	45 minutes
240,000 BTU/hr	30 minutes

Fall Conditions

Raising the water in the hot tub from 75° F. to 105° F.
Heat required: 192,000 BTU

Type of Heater	Time Required to 105° F.
60,000 BTU/hr	3 hours
120,000 BTU/hr	1 1/2 hours
180,000 BTU/hr	1 hour
240,000 BTU/hr	45 minutes

Winter Conditions

Raising the water in the hot tub from 55° F. to 105° F.
Heat required: 330,000 BTU

Type of Heater	Time Required to 105° F.
60,000 BTU/hr	5 hours and 30 minutes
120,000 BTU/hr	2 hours and 45 minutes
180,000 BTU/hr	1 hour and 50 minutes
240,000 BTU/hr	1 hour and 24 minutes

The Pump

By shopping around as we did you ought to be able to pick up a used water pump for about $10. Used water pumps are even more plentiful than used gas heaters.

A one-horsepower pump can circulate 80 gallons of water per minute. Therefore in ten minutes' time, the entire tubful of hot water can be pumped through the plumbing "loop" (tub, water pump, chlorinator, heater, tub) one time.

In addition to pumping the water through the loop, your pump has a second function—to power the hydro-massage jets. For each jet you add to your hot tub, your pump needs to generate from 1/3- to 1/2-horsepower. A water pump of one-horsepower therefore provides enough power to pump 80 gallons of water per minute *and* to activate *two* hydrojet units.

Incidentally, the use of solar panels eliminates the need for any kind of water pump. A solar energy system can be made to function on the "thermosyphon" principle where hot water is made to flow through the tub and collectors by situating the collectors at different levels and linking both tub and collector across a gradient drop of at least one foot. The practical matter of installing a solar collector is dealt with in a later chapter.

The Filter

A Diatomaceous Earth filter should be installed between the pump and heater. The filter serves to keep the water in the hot tub free of impurities and crystal clear. Moreover, it keeps the plumbing from clogging and acts to prevent corrosion.

The D.E. filter consists of a stainless steel housing and an inner webbing of microscopic green algae. It is an ecologically sound water filter and will protect your hot tub system as well as any filter. A pressure gauge on top of the tank allows you to monitor the water pressure in the system. Water pressure should be kept between 15 and 20 pounds per square inch when the pump is operating.

The filter may be cleaned periodically by unclamping the housing around the base of the filter, removing the comb

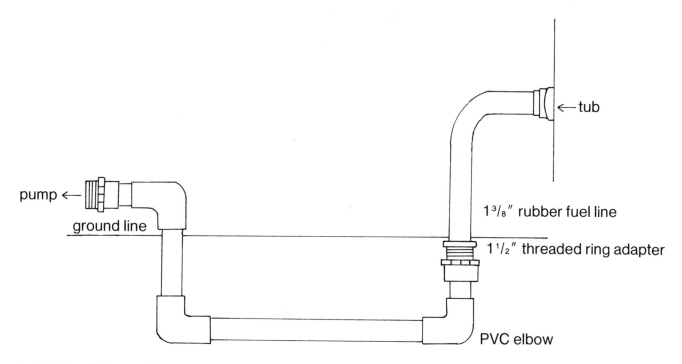

Plumbing your hot tub: tub outlet to pump inlet.

tub

$1^3/_8$" rubber fuel line

$1^1/_2$" threaded ring adapter

PVC elbow

pump ←

ground line

inside and washing it thoroughly with a garden hose.

You may, if you wish, add a chlorinator to the support system to keep the water clean in appearance. It serves to supply a pre-measured amount of chlorine to the hot tub system as the

tub is used. It is just as easy, however, to throw in a few grams of powdered chlorine every week or so by hand and stir it around until it dissolves. Incidentally, wait at least two hours after chlorinating your hot tub before getting into the water.

(1) Tub Outlet to Pump Inlet

Start the plumbing connections with a 12-inch piece of $1^3/_8$-inch rubber fuel line. Fit one end around the tub outlet and the other end into a $1^1/_2$-inch threaded PVC ring adapter which allows you to telescope to a larger

Use rubber fuel line from the tub outlet to the pump and bury the line to conceal the plumbing.

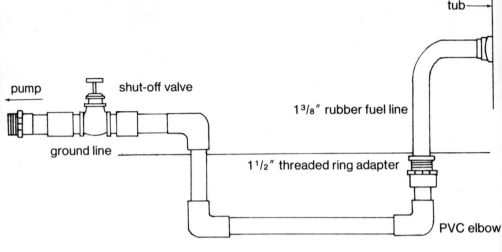

A shut-off valve should be installed between tub and support system as shown above.

diameter (1½-inch) pipe. Continue the line below ground (to conceal the plumbing) and fit a relevant number of elbows and straight sections of PVC which lead to the inlet of the pump. You need not plumb these connections exactly the way we did. You may, for instance, design your own method of connecting the loop by using more rubber fuel line, fewer elbows, more straight pipe etc. The important thing is

that the essential structures (pump, heater, filter, tub, jets) are connected in the correct series. *How* you accomplish the connections is up to you.

We feel it is a good idea to install a shut-off valve between the tub and support system. It will permit you to repair or clean any part of the equipment (such as the filter) while the

water is turned off. (Without the valve in the line, you would have to resort to placing a rubber strip against the outlet valve on the inside wall of the tub, where the water pressure would hold the strip in place.) The drawing on this page shows one method of installing the valve, in case you have used rubber fuel line or buried a portion of the line beneath the ground. The drawing on page 71 will provide

Use a small butane torch to heat the solder and pipe.

you with an alternative, especially if you are planning to use solar energy.

(2) Pump to Filter

Cut off a length of 1⅜-inch copper pipe or PVC and brush on some soldering paste. Use a pipe cutter for copper pipe or a hand saw for PVC. If you use PVC, you may eliminate the soldering process and substitute a liquid welding material designed to be used with this kind of pipe. Using a hand-held butane torch or equivalent heat source, heat the pipe at the point of connection until the solder melts when placed in contact with the pipe. Run the tip of the solder around the joint until it completely seals the connection.

Soldering paste for copper connections. You could use PVC for all plumbing connections.

A hand-held pipe cutter for cutting copper plumbing.

Pump-to-filter connection.

The filter-to-heater connection in place. Assembling the heater outlet-to-tub line.

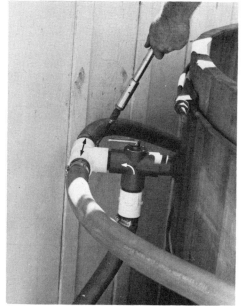

Secure the hydrojets using ordinary auto radiator clamps.

(3) Filter to Heater

Study the photo at left, then fit a relevant number of straight sections of pipe and elbows and join them to make the filter-to-heater connection. Repeat the previous procedures if soldering the joints.

(4) Heater Outlet to Tub Inlet

Fit an elbow into the heater outlet. Insert a straight piece of pipe to connect with a section of flexible rubber fuel line. Run the fuel line up to the tub inlet/hydrojet assembly. Use ordinary auto radiator clamps to secure both ends of the rubber fuel line. You will find it less cumbersome to bury the longer section of pipe a foot or so below ground, in the same way that earlier, the pump inlet was connected to the tub. The plumbing "loop" is now complete.

The complete plumbing "loop."

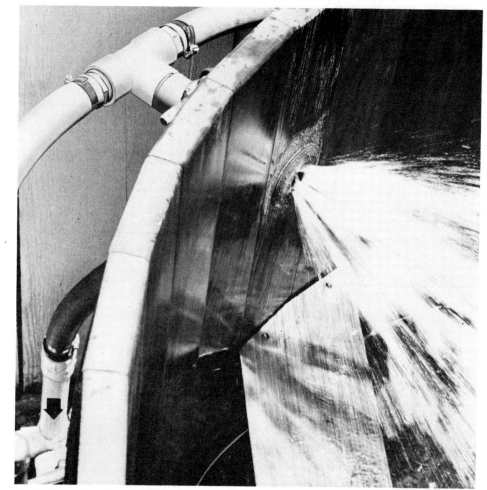

Testing the entire tub assembly.

(5) Hydrojets

All that now remains is to hook up the lines at the tub itself. Connect a section of rubber line from one side of the manifold tee to the first jet. Repeat the same procedure and, using a clamp, hook up the second jet. Be sure to check that all of the plumbing connections are complete before turning on the system.

LEACHING, CHLORINE AND pH

Keeping the water in your hot tub fresh and clean-looking makes for more enjoyable tubbing.

Leaching the Hot Tub

Redwood contains tannic acid and when the wood is wet it gives off a reddish residue. Before the tub has been leached this residue will ooze from the walls of the tub and give the water an oily, brackish appearance. To leach this residue from the wood, fill the tub with water, add two or three pounds of soda ash, stir it up, and allow the mixture to sit for a few days. Then open the hose bib and drain the tub. Refill the tub with fresh water and the tub is now ready to operate.

Chlorine

Chlorine powder will keep the water in the tub fresh and clean looking. If you wish to chlorinate, add two to three teaspoons of powdered chlorine to the tub every two weeks. In addition to keeping the water fresh looking, it also serves to disinfect the tub. Wait a few hours to allow the chlorine to thoroughly dissolve before getting into the tub.

pH Factor

The pH factor is not only a term to describe your shampoo. pH (meaning potential of hydrogen) is commonly used by chemists to describe the acid and alkaline balance of a liquid. An improper pH balance will result in the formation of certain algae on the walls and floor of the tub. Worse still, a severe imbalance will lead to corrosion in the pipes, filter, pump and heater.

It is well worth the few dollars to buy a pH test kit at a spa dealer or through a plumbing supply catalog and conduct periodic checks on the water in your tub. Proper pH means an acid balance of from 7.5 to 7.9 and alkalinity, 125 pph (parts per hundred).

Chapter 6

SOLARIZING THE HOT TUB

Tools Needed to Solarize Your Hot Tub

☐ Hammer and chisel

☐ Shovel (or post hole digger)

☐ Small butane torch for soldering

☐ Screwdriver

☐ Wire brush to clean soldered joints

☐ Hand or power saw

☐ Pliers

☐ Crescent wrench

☐ Portable electric hand drill and 2⁵/₁₆-inch hole saw

Building Materials Needed to Solarize Your Hot Tub

☐ Two flat-plate solar collectors

☐ 36 feet of 4 by 4-inch "construction" grade redwood.

☐ Eight 3-inch wood screws with bolt ends.

☐ Assortment of nails.

☐ 2⁵/₁₆-inch hot water inlet assembly (PVC).

☐ 2⁵/₁₆-inch cold water suction drain assembly (PVC).

☐ One-inch PVC pipe.

☐ One-inch shut-off valve.

☐ ³/₈-inch copper tubing.

Note: The amount of PVC and copper tubing you will need for the job will depend entirely on the distance you place your collectors from the tub. It is a good idea to plan your plumbing loop on paper and estimate as closely as you can the amount of both copper tubing and PVC you will need.

☐ Assortment of one-inch PVC and ³/₈-inch copper elbows, ells and tees with which to assemble the two way hot/cold water line from tub to collector.

☐ Pressure-release valve.

☐ ½ pint PVC liquid weld.

The Investment

Solar energy is no longer an impractical way of powering or heating our homes and industry. Even though solar equipment represents an initially more costly investment, this investment should be looked at over an extended period of time in order to weigh its actual cost to you.

Think of it this way: if you purchase a new gas heater, you still have to pay for the gas that it burns; however, once you have paid for your solar panels, that is the end of it—no escalating fuel bills to worry about, no overdue statements from Con-Ed, no fuel shortages to fear. Moreover, with proper installation, you can heat up your hot tub to 105 degrees F. every day year in and year out for absolutely nothing—that is, without using any fuel other than the sun's energy.

Furthermore, the chances of something going wrong with your solar energy equipment are virtually non-existent by comparison with any of the

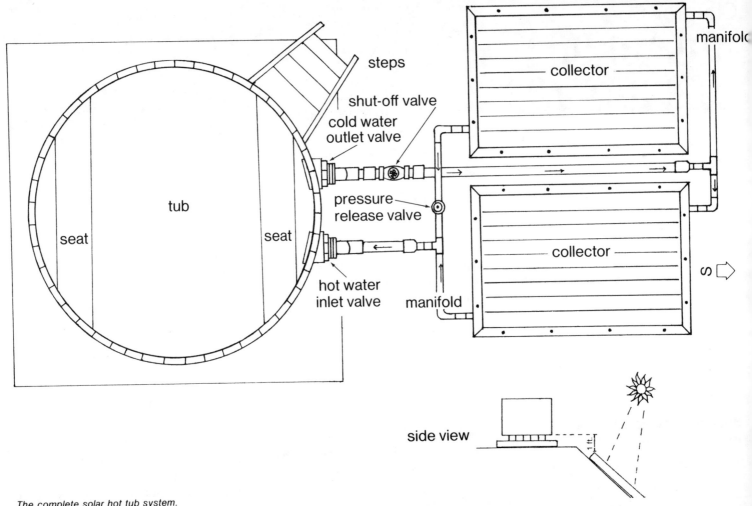

manifold

steps

shut-off valve

cold water
outlet valve

tub

pressure
release valve

seat

seat

collector

collector

S

hot water
inlet valve

manifold

side view

1 ft.

The complete solar hot tub system.

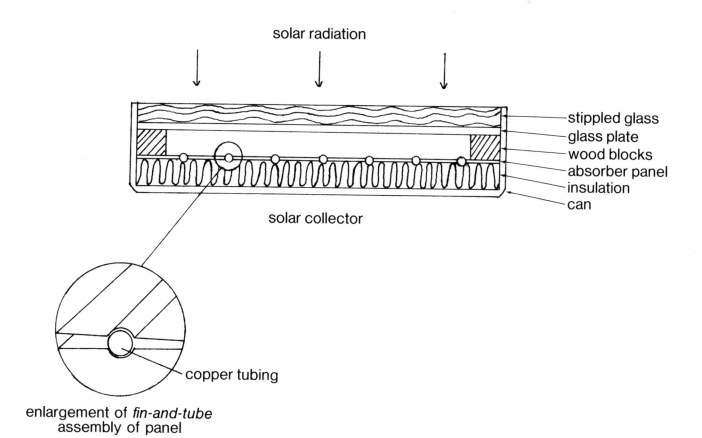

solar radiation

solar collector

stippled glass
glass plate
wood blocks
absorber panel
insulation
can

copper tubing

enlargement of *fin-and-tube*
assembly of panel

How a solar collector works.

conventional equipment using ordinary fossil fuels.

Tax Credits

There is another sound reason for "going solar" at the present time. Some thirty state governments now offer some kind of "solar tax credit" to consumers who elect to use solar energy to power some part of their home. In California, for instance, you can deduct *up to 55 percent of the cost* of your solar energy system from your state income tax. This tax credit, moreover, is valid for up to a $3,000 purchase of solar energy equipment.

Anyone may apply for the solar tax credit in California by writing to the Franchise Tax Board and requesting Form 3805L. Those who live in other states may inquire about the solar tax credit by writing to their local tax boards or by contacting their state representatives.

Selecting the Solar Panels

The kind of solar collector which you might use to heat your hot tub consists of a strong steel casing called the "can." The can is lined with heavy-duty asbestos which supports a flat-plate aluminum panel (called the "fin") through which copper tubing runs. This "fin-and-tube" assembly is the heart of a solar collector. It is painted black with a special selective paint designed to maximize absorption of solar radiation.

One or two panes of heavy stippled (etched) glass permit the collector to act as a heat trap—the sun's rays easily pass through the glass but once inside are unable to pass back out. The narrow copper tubing which is pressed between the aluminum fins of the collector panel is heated by simple conduction from contact with the fins. The water flowing through the tubing is heated to the desired temperature (105 degrees F.) and passes through the entire collector and up into the hot tub.

An interesting fact about a solar collector is that it is able to function perfectly well on a hazy day when the sky is overcast, in summer or in the middle of winter, or even on a cloudy day (although thick clouds *will* inhibit its operation). The sun need not be "visible" in the open sky to power the collector. It is rather through the invisible rays of the sun—the solar radiation—that the solar panel is heated. Incidentally, a shut-off valve should be installed between the tub and the collector to stop the flow of water through the collector at night. Unless this is done, a "reverse flow" will begin and the collector will quickly radiate heat to the night sky, to outer space where the temperature is minus 50 degrees Fahrenheit. You will thus lose much of the heat in your hot tub which otherwise might be saved until the next day.

The Thermosyphon

The solar collector and the hot tub work in tandem on the "thermosyphon" principle. Cold water naturally sinks to the bottom of your tub and hot water rises to the surface. Hence, by positioning the tub above the solar panels (at least one foot above), a set of displacements will be made to take place, causing cold water to flow down into the collectors and hot water up into the tub. The solar panels will act as a natural regulator; once the water in the collectors becomes hot, it will rise to the level of the tub. The cycle is continuous as long as both cold and

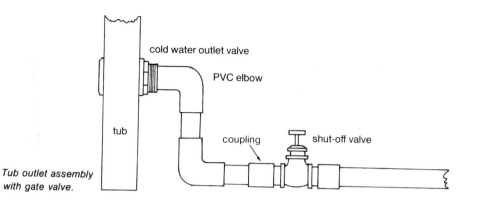

cold water outlet valve

PVC elbow

tub

coupling

shut-off valve

Tub outlet assembly with gate valve.

Solar plumbing.

hot water lines between the collector and tub are kept open.

The Collector Angle

With minor variations dependent upon the latitude of your site, you should install your solar panels at a 45 degree angle facing south. This orientation will enable you to harvest maximum solar radiation in summer as well as in winter, when the sun is lower in the sky.

The Site

The ideal site for your solar collectors is in open terrain where there are no obstructions—overhanging branches, a roof gable, telephone lines—to cause shadows to be cast on the surface of the collectors during the hours of 10 a.m. until 4 p.m., the hours of maximum solar radiation each day.

If you intend to utilize the "thermo-syphon" principle and dispense with the use of a water pump and hydrojets, you will have to place the solar collectors at least a foot below the floor of the hot tub; therefore, some kind of gradient is necessary whether natural or man-made.

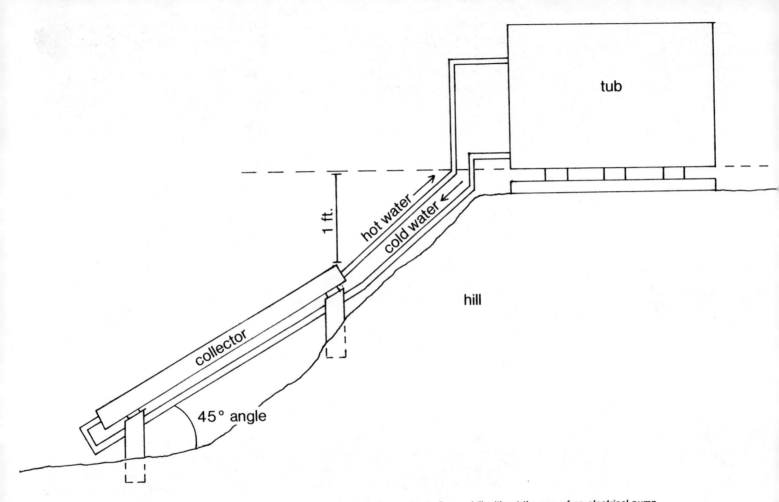

tub

1 ft.

hot water

cold water

hill

collector

45° angle

Thermosyphon. A way to use free heat for your hot tub and to cause the hot water to flow uphill without the use of an electrical pump.

Constructing a solar rack. Notch the end of each wooden post with a chisel.

The solar rack.

The Solar Rack

It is a good idea to build a rack to support the panels (they weigh about 100 pounds each). Your collector should face south and be tilted at an angle of 45 degrees—an orientation which is a good average for harvesting both the high summer and low winter sun. For the amateur astronomer who wishes to change the angle of his collectors each month to maximize the solar harvest, an adjustable extension can be added to the rack which will permit raising and lowering of the collectors.

Using a hammer and chisel cut a notch one inch deep in the end of each of four 4 by 4-inch wooden posts as shown. In addition, bevel the top of each of these posts to an angle of 45 degrees. Dig four holes at the site and sink the posts to a depth of two feet. It is a good idea to paint the posts with creosote to prevent them from rotting. Use a level and school protractor to see that all the posts are perfectly vertical and that the bevel is a true 45 degree angle. Mix up a small quantity of cement and pack the cement around the base of the 4 by 4 posts. Next, nail two sections of 4 by 4 across each pair of posts as shown and use wood screws with bolt ends to secure the collectors in position on the rack.

The solar rack in place.

Placing the first solar panel on the rack.

Installing a second panel on the rack.

Hooking Up the Tub to the Collectors

It is assumed that you have already installed the floor drain and hose bib connections as demonstrated earlier.

You now need to drill two additional holes in the side of the tub for the hot water inlet and cold water outlet ports. Insert a "hole saw" in your drill to drill two $2^5/_{16}$-inch holes, one 26 inches above the floor for the hot water inlet,

the second, eight inches above the floor for the cold water port.

The amount of copper plumbing or PVC you need to plumb the job depends entirely on the distance from tub to collector panels.

Install a suction drain assembly using Teflon tape and liquid weld (PVC "weld-on") at the base of the tub. Follow the same procedure when installing the inlet for the hot water. Next, put together a relevant set of PVC straight sections and elbows to extend from the side of the tub to the collectors.

The Collector Manifold

Each solar collector requires a cold and hot water connection. To link both cold water inlets at the collector as well as both hot water outlets, construct a manifold (a funnel, really) of $3/_8$-inch copper tubing and an appropriate number of tees and couplings as shown. Manifolds at both ends of the collectors will thus permit the collectors to function as a single unit. Connect the cold water inlet and hot water outlet of the collector manifold to the hot and cold water lines extending from the tub as shown.

Solar hot and cold lines as they leave solar collector.

Making a "header" to link two solar panels.

It would be wise to install a "pressure relief" valve in the hot water line and as near the collector as possible. This valve will operate only when steam pressure in the system exceeds the heat limit for which the collectors have been designed. Some collectors, however, already have such a pressure-relief system built into them. To test the system simply open the shut-off valve, allow the water from the tub to run down into the collectors and let the sun put everything to work!

View of solar hot and cold lines.

Chapter 7
WINTERIZING THE HOT TUB

The Hot Tub and Winter

There is no reason why a hot tub cannot be built and enjoyed in a winter climate. Naturally for the eight or nine months of the year when temperatures stay above freezing, your hot tub will function just as well as if it were sitting in Miami or San Francisco. But when the mercury drops to freezing and ice begins to form you will have to prepare yourself and your hot tub for it.

When it begins to really get cold, set the thermostat on your tub to 50 degrees F. and leave it there until spring except for the times when you turn it up to 105 degrees or higher and go hot tubbing.

Build a wooden cover and keep it on the tub when it is not in use. If you haven't placed the heater, pump and filter indoors or in some kind of shed, build a simple wooden box lined with ordinary insulation and cover the pump and filter to keep snow and ice out of the machinery.

If you haven't buried the plumbing pipes well below the frost line, at least place them within a series of square boxes lined with tar paper (a reliable Vermont remedy) to insulate them from the cold.

There may be a moment or two of chilly discomfort when scurrying from the back door across the snowdrifts to climb into your tub (wear a woolen robe)—actually, it's no worse than jumping into a cold ocean on a hot summer's day—but once you sink those bones of yours and that tired, aching body into that hot, bubbling, steaming brew, you will feel yourself come alive and know the run was worth it.

And when you step out, guess what? That cold won't bother you one bit! But don't be *too* confident. Either get back in the tub or make for the house. You don't want to catch cold.

Now that you are officially a hot tubber, you know that it beats the boredom of jogging (it's just as good for you), calisthenics (ugh!) or fighting the lift lines at the ski resort (too expensive anyway). Fifteen minutes or a half hour in that hot tub in January will give you a lift to make you feel as if summer had come back to stay.

A GLOSSARY OF TERMS

The Modern Cooper's Glossary

B.T.U.   The amount of heat required to raise one pound of water one degree Fahrenheit.

COOPERAGE   The art of constructing tubs without the use of glue, nails or dowels, using wooden staves and iron hoops.

CHINES   The 4 by 4-inch wooden "spines" used to support the hot tub, placed between the tub bottom and the concrete foundation.

CUDDLE (OR LOVE) TUB   A small hot tub for two (i.e. 3 by 3 feet in diameter) and occasionally placed indoors.

DIATOMACEOUS EARTH   The term used to describe a natural water filter used by ecologically-minded hot tubbers, made of microscopic particles of green algae.

DADO (GROOVE, SLOT OR CROZE)   The narrow cut at the base of a cooper's stave by which to join the staves to the floor of the hot tub.

FUN GUN   A small (and in our opinion, dangerous) water pistol manufactured by some cooperages which can be connected to the hot water inlet of the tub. Feels great when striking any other parts of the human anatomy but the eyeballs.

HOOPS AND LUGS   Steel or wrought-iron bands (*hoops*) which encircle the hot tub and hold the staves in place; the aluminum or steel blocks (*lugs*) which serve to connect the hoops.

HOT TUB   A large wooden tub made of redwood staves and hoops, supported on a concrete base and fed with hot water (to 105 degrees F.) pumped from a gas or solar heater through high pressure hydromassage jets in the sides (staves) of the tub.

pH (potential of Hydrogen)   The term used to describe the acid-alkaline balance of water in your hot tub.

PVC (Poly-Vinyl-Chloride)   A tough, lightweight, inexpensive, easy-to-use plastic pipe which we strongly suggest that you use to plumb your tub. PVC is readily obtainable through a number of well-known suppliers such as Sears or Montgomery-Ward. Believe it or not, the plumbing section in the Ward catalog is actually a marvelous trip through a prosaic world.

REDWOOD   The best wood with which to build your hot tub. Light, dry, with extraordinary expansion characteristics, redwood makes superlatively tight, waterproof joints. While less expensive woods can be used to make your hot tub, redwood is the cooper's dream!

SOLAR COLLECTOR   An excellent type of heater for your hot tub. Solar collectors are wonderful machines (without moving parts or fuel) with which to harvest solar energy. Consists of a panel made of copper tubing pressed between aluminum fins; the panel is supported on a layer of asbestos and enclosed within twin panes of glass which act as a heat "trap"—allowing the sun's rays to enter the collector and to be used to heat the panel. The sun need not be visible in the sky to "collect" solar energy. It is the invisible radiation which activates the collector and heats the water.

STAVES   The upright redwood slats which form the sides or walls of the hot tub.

THERMOSYPHON   The automatic (no pump needed) flow of cold water from the tub downhill to the solar collector(s) where it is heated and then displaced upward and into the tub. To utilize the thermosyphon effect, the base of the tub must be placed at least one foot above the top of the solar collectors.

VASODILATION   One of the many therapeutic benefits of the hot tub—the enlargement of blood vessels in the body of a person soaking in the hot tub and the corresponding increase in venous and arterial circulation.

INDEX

THE INTERNATIONAL DESSERT BOOK

by Goldye Mullen. This collection of over 120 extraordinary recipes from around the world attempts to restore to its rightful place that maligned and misunderstood portion of the meal —the *special* dessert for the festive occasion. Illustrated by Fuzzzy. $7.95 paper, $10.95 cloth

WHAT COLOR IS YOUR PARACHUTE? *A Practical Manual for Job-Hunters & Career-Changers*

by Richard Nelson Bolles. A new, completely revised edition of this established best-selling title tells in step-by-step detail how to identify what you want to do with the rest of your life, how to locate the job you want, and how to convince the employer you are the best person for the job. Illustrated. $5.95 paper, $9.95 cloth. .

HOW TO GROW MORE VEGETABLES*

*Than You Ever Thought Possible on Less Land Than You Can Imagine

by John Jeavons. Ten Speed Press is proud to present a new edition of a book first published in 1974 by Ecology Action of the Midpeninsula, about the Biodynamic/French Intensive Method of gardening. "The Method" has produced yields of from four to six times the national average of US agriculture with about one-half the water use, with no chemicals and a hundredth of the energy consumption of commercial agriculture. A backyard gardener, with less than two hundred square feet per person, could grow a year's supply of soft fruits and vegetables, with about ten minutes a day required for upkeep! "... the best plain-language explanation of Biodynamic/French Intensive gardening techniques we've yet seen."—*Mother Earth News.* "could revolutionize small gardening..."—*The Washington Post* Illustrated. $5.95 paper, $8.95 cloth

ANYBODY'S BIKE BOOK

by Tom Cuthbertson. This newly revised and enlarged half-million copy bestseller has become a classic manual for owners and buyers of 1-speed, 3-speed, and 10-speed bikes. Illustrated by Rick Morrall. $3.95 paper, $7.95 cloth.

I CAN SWIM YOU CAN SWIM

by Tom Cuthbertson and Lee Cole. This simple guide demonstrates how anyone can learn to swim, regardless of abilities and in spite of past experiences with water. Step-by-step exercises are given which allow you to overcome fears, to feel comfortable and to enjoy yourself in the water. Fully illustrated. $3 paper.

HONEY FEAST

by Gene Opton and Nancie Hughes. More than 100 recipes from around the world include appetizers, meat and vegetable dishes as well as the breads, sweets and savories which honey has long been famous for. $3.95 paper, $7.95 cloth.

HOUSE PLANTS: A New Primer for a Dumb Thumb

by Nancy Roca. Here is a revised and updated edition of one of the best of the house plant books directed at the kind of people who have not had any luck with plants. Basic guidelines for choosing and caring for a wide variety of the most common houseplants. $3.95 paper.

THE MALT-EASE FLAGON

by R. O. Despain. Incredibly informative, yet easy-to-understand guide to brewing beer at home. Begins with equipment, provides recipes *for* beer, *with* beer, and ends with lists of mail-order outfits, "the IRS", and tables of measurements. $4.95 paper, $8.95 cloth.

THE MOOSEWOOD COOKBOOK

by Mollie Katzen. "One of the most attractive, least dogmatic meatless cookbooks printed— an engaging blend of hand lettered care and solid food information...."—Bob Heisler, *The New York Post.* $7.95 paper, $9.95 cloth.

Please include $.50 additional for each paperback, or $.75 each clothbound copy, for postage and handling.

 TEN SPEED PRESS, Box 7123, Berkeley, California 94707